That Someone You Will Never Want To Meet

PALMETTO
PUBLISHING
Charleston, SC
www.PalmettoPublishing.com

Hardcover ISBN: 9798822961913
Paperback ISBN: 9798822961920
eBook ISBN: 9798822961937

That Someone You Will Never Want To Meet

Sandra Russell Wadsworth

A Personal
Story of
Rape and
Its Bizarre
Aftermath

Contents

Introduction

Upon exiting the car that New Year's Eve in 1978, I immediately felt that something was off. Where were the sounds of the fireworks that usually permeated the night air on any given New Year's Eve? Eerily noticeable as well was the complete absence of the continual barking from the dogs in the neighborhood one could always count on, fireworks or not.

Earlier in the evening, I had stopped by my parents' house for dinner. It had already begun to get dark outside as we were finishing dinner, so my mama suggested I just stay the night with them and go home in the morning. I declined her offer with the lame excuse that I had some long-overdue laundry waiting for me at home that couldn't wait.

Little did I know I would live to regret not taking Mama up on that invitation.

In just a few hours, a certain someone, through vile and meticulous planning, would set into motion a heinous crime of rape at gunpoint. The individual's inhumane and wanton sense of self-entitlement and depravity would exact upon another an ocean of torment, trauma, and scars, which would require a life's investment of time in which to fade. The recall of the events that occurred on that horrific night would cast a permanent, long-suffering shadow of terror and fear by rewinding and replaying in my mind like scenes repeatedly rehearsed over and over in a horror movie. That single, solitary event on that frigid, wintry night would forever destroy the very core of a human being, along with all dignity, security, and independence of a life previously lived.

PART I: MY LIFE BEFORE

Chapter One:
A Night Interrupted

I could never understand why on *that* particular night I was smitten with an acute sense of fatigue never before experienced, accompanied by an exaggerated form of sleepiness. I later reasoned that this unique phenomenon, together with the silent, albeit bewitching, air encompassing the atmosphere that night, played a defining role in the ability of that certain someone to inject himself into my personal life forever.

Whatever the reasons, I didn't hear a thing until it was too late.

My true-life horror movie began with an unrehearsed script—at least on my part—wherein the director signaled the first act to begin. The on-set props would be the musty, putrid smell of cigarette smoke encircling the main character, and the only background sounds would appear to be low, counterfeit breathing emitting from the main character, who was also the director of the movie, upon his entrance.

Chapter Two:
Someone's Presence

The feature begins with a certain someone leaning over me and breathing into my ear. In an instant, all of my thoughts, senses, and emotions catapulted into frenzied chaos and calamity as if I had been violently thrust onto a predisposed collision course with no sense of direction. My thoughts seemed to crash and intertwine with each other, almost to the point of strangulation, and the normal breathing pattern that existed prior to that moment abruptly came to a halt then temporarily began again, allowing only the shallowest puffs of air to escape.

As if divinely installed at birth, an otherwise dormant instinct of self-preservation kicked in, sending my mind and body into what I can only describe as a state of shock and paralysis for my protection. At the same time, a flurry of incoherent and irrational thoughts spiraled out of control and sequence, stumbling over each other, attempting abandonment. I felt as though I was uncontrollably spinning counterclockwise on a carousel ride, unable to function in any capacity, let alone exit. I also found myself unable to open my eyes or react physically in any manner whatsoever. Engulfed in sheer fright and terror, I could feel my heart pounding so intensely that it felt as though it was on the outside of my chest, that it had somehow escaped the warm, fleshy chamber it previously occupied. There had to be some sort of internal protective mechanism miraculously implanted at birth to keep one's heart from permanently ceasing to beat. There were times throughout the night that it truly felt as though my heart had, in fact, arbitrarily removed itself from my being.

Then came a vague rendition of a thought that somehow grappled existence, which bade me to cry out, to scream, to do *something*, while at the same time, my conscience negated that directive, telling me to remain perfectly still, not to move, to keep my eyes closed and pretend I was still sleeping.

Chapter Three:
The Sound of That Someone's Breathing

I was asleep in bed when I first became aware of that certain someone's presence, only by the sound of his breathing. It seemed as if that someone had been leaning over me, watching me sleep for a time, since there remained a steady lingering odor of someone who had been smoking recently. The breathing began relatively slow, muffled, and calm; however, it rapidly graduated to an erratic, heavier, raspy tone, clearly indicative of a lifetime of chain-smoking. That someone's very presence reeked of cigarette smoke and ash so repugnant that I quickly became nauseated and felt as though I might vomit, faint, or both. I've always wished that I would have, in fact, fainted in order to escape the knowledge of what was evidently going to happen, along with the terror of thinking that my life was about to end.

I was emphatically cold and numb all over, helpless, with a lack of control over my extremities. All sense of feeling had vacated my arms and legs, as if my limbs had simply been attached to my body as an afterthought. I had become this ineffectual rag doll lying on a bed to be tossed about and discarded at will. It was soon to become very apparent that any attempts on my part to try to convince that certain someone I was still sleeping would all be in vain and that what was left of the real me would soon be whisked away and vanish like a vapor that exits the earth.

Chapter Four:
Physical Contact

I tried to convince myself that, if I could remain perfectly still with my eyes closed, that someone would think I didn't hear the breathing, which had somehow gained momentum, turning into a lustful, gasping rhythm. I began praying that the someone would simply take what he wanted from the house and just go. I came to the realization that my plan was not going to work the moment he began stroking my hair. At that point all of the heat previously warming my body dissipated, leaving me a frozen berg of ice. In what seemed like just seconds later, the someone savagely grabbed me by my hair while simultaneously dragging me out of bed. He then pressed something solid and cold—I assumed it was a gun—against the skin of my neck. I didn't have to wait very long for confirmation of my assumption, as next I heard that someone bellow out the words, "If you scream, I'll blow your head off."

I had often heard those exact words verbalized in the past by various actors in movies, never once imagining I would someday hear them directed at me personally, and this was definitely not a movie! Upon hearing those words in the manner and tone in which they were delivered, my thoughts again were sent hurling into oblivion. There were various limited and labored thoughts and words that attempted to make their way to the forefront of my mind, seeking understanding only to slightly resurrect in the way of a blurry fog. I had difficulty in distinguishing real thoughts from the fabricated. Unwillingly, I had been thrust into an overpowering inhuman realm of evil that I never knew existed, all the while never knowing if that certain someone was going to follow through with the words he'd just uttered.

I could feel my personality and character being voided and extracted, never to be regained. I was traversing down a barbarous, ruthless pathway with an unknown ending. It then began to slowly sink in that the someone had not come to steal from me but to rape, and he now controlled the outcome of what remained of the rest of me from my previous life. He controlled all of my movements from that point forward by continually and mercilessly pulling and grasping me by my hair while making sure he kept the gun pressed into my neck. The callous and vengeful behavior along with the language exhibited by this someone reflected a long-standing rage, hatred, and malevolent disdain and animosity toward women in general, and on this particular night, I had become the chosen vessel in which he would enact his plan of revenge.

Chapter Five:
Former Life

I was born in 1954 and raised by parents who were very private individuals and very protective of their children. This mode of living resulted in me and my siblings growing up in a vastly sheltered environment up to and throughout our teenage years. Our parents did not discuss personal issues with us and certainly not any that were sexual in nature. Our parents also did not discuss political, social, or criminal issues that may have been going on in the world around us. Our parents kept up with the affairs of the world by watching the news and reading the local newspaper. My siblings and I were not the least bit interested in what Walter Cronkite had to say, so we never listened to the news ourselves. Our sporadic and limited viewing pleasure consisted pretty much of *The Red Skelton Show*, *The Little Rascals*, country-Western movies, and at times, *The Ed Sullivan Show*, depending on who he had on his show as guests. We watched cartoons on Saturdays and went to church on Sundays and Wednesdays, with church having played a significant role in our lives.

There was one occasion when the Beatles were on *The Ed Sullivan Show* for the first time, and to our shock and surprise, we were allowed to watch. The whole time we were watching, I kept thinking that any time now, Daddy's going to walk over and turn off the television or, at the very least, change the channel. The only thing I could think of was that Daddy may have been a little curious about what the crying, screaming, and fainting exhibited by all the teenage girls when they saw the Beatles was all about.

It may come as a surprise to some people that anyone could have grown up in a sheltered environment as we did, especially when you think of life as we know it today. One has to consider that the time we lived in—the 1960s and 1970s—and our specific circumstances were vastly different, almost as if we had grown up in another era. We were not allowed to go places or do things that young people do now at a very early age, and even when we were allowed to participate in the very minimalist of events, there were always strict limitations and rules that applied. Today's social media, cell phones, flat-screen TVs, and computers, just to mention a few, were nonexistent back then. Our family had one landline telephone located in the main room of the house that was part of a shared telephone line called a party line. This strategically located telephone awarded no opportunity for kids or teens to carry on conversations without parents being able to monitor and supervise.

We understood that our parents were trying to protect us from the bad things going on in the world and could do so while we were living under their roof. Sadly, after removing myself from under that roof of protection, I would become a victim of the bad things going on in the world. I sometimes think that it may have been better for me to have known about all those certain someones running around loose in the world, creating havoc with all their animalistic, uncontrollable urges.

As a young, socially inept girl at the time, I thought I knew everything necessary for living the "adult life." However, I would find out in the worst possible way that a plethora of issues that I knew absolutely nothing about existed outside my parents' environment. I was extremely naive, but I didn't realize I was naive at the time; after all, you can't be naive about something you don't know about.

At the time of my rape, I lived alone in an area located off Hickory Grove Road in Gaston County, North Carolina. I was living an independent and secure life—or so I thought—in that miniscule space I called my home, and the thought never entered my mind that I was placing myself in a position of risk or danger by living alone. It would take one unforeseeable event on one single night to obliterate and erase all my prior beliefs and trust in the goodness of mankind and the world, in general, that I was brought up in. As a result, I would never again be the person I once was, and subsequently, I became an unknown certain someone.

I was not aware of the criminal element that existed throughout the world while living within the confines of my family's environment. I didn't understand that, when I left my parents' home, embarking on a life of my own, the environment that had protected me since birth and up to that point ended when I moved out of my parents' home.

After I was raped, the soul and spirit that had previously existed within me was forever altered. I had been forced to learn, at the hands of an animal who walked upright, that the world I lived in all of my life was not the *real* world at all. Never again would I be that Sandy who was born to Lamar and Julia or the Sandy who shared her childhood with her sister and two brothers, the cheerleader from Arlington Junior High, or the Sandy that graduated from Hunter Huss High School in 1972.

Chapter Six:
Hours Leading Up to the Rape

I was working at Eckerd Drugs at the time of the rape, and after work on that particular evening, I decided to drop by my parents' house, hoping to make it in time for one of Mama's homecooked meals. Since Mama never liked the idea of any of her children driving at night, no matter how old they were, and since it had already begun to get dark outside, she suggested that I just stay with them for the night. How quickly I had forgotten that old saying that mothers always know what's best.

After leaving my parents' house and arriving home that night, I started some laundry that I had forever been putting off. Prior to the laundry completely drying, however, I began to experience a rare and unique sense of fatigue and sleepiness, as I have mentioned, so I decided to go to bed. I removed the laundry from the dryer and placed it on an ironing board I had set up in my spare bedroom to finish drying.

I had always been a light sleeper, and seldom did I sleep soundly through an entire night. I will never be able to explain why on that particular night, I didn't stumble through my boring, predictable, and repetitive nighttime routine, which consisted of tossing and turning in bed, getting up for a bathroom visit, getting up to get something to drink, or if I couldn't go back to sleep, debating whether to read, listen to music, or watch some late-night TV. It defies all logic that, having participated in this steady, nightly bedtime routine practically all of my life, on the night in question, I would be found in such a deep sleep.

It was discovered by the police on the night I was raped that the window in my spare bedroom located at the other end of the house was partially open and the outside screen was barely hanging in track. The window's screen frame was bent on both sides, the retaining hooks were on the outside of the track, and the window screen had been cut as well. That someone had also turned a drum-type trash can on its side and placed it underneath the window, allowing him to crawl inside without making any noise. In addition, the someone, either on that night or sometime previously, had placed cement blocks on their sides underneath the back door.

PART II: THAT SOMEONE'S ATTACK

Chapter Seven:
The Rape

After the certain someone had pulled me out of the bed by my hair, he belted out, "You got any money?"

I responded, "In my pocketbook on the kitchen table."

While still holding on to me by my hair, the gun still pressed into my neck, that someone shoved me into the kitchen, ordering me to get the money. I removed the few dollars I had in my billfold and handed it to him over my shoulder. He became instantly enraged, forcibly jerking my head backward, and blurting out, "This all you got?"

We remained standing in the kitchen for a few seconds, and I sensed that he was gazing around the kitchen. I then heard him jerk the telephone cord from my kitchen wall phone before shoving me back into the bedroom. He then ordered me to get a pillowcase from the bed, put it over my head, and get on my knees. It was at this point I could see that the someone was wearing a dark ski mask and dark gloves that had a leather-like feel to them. I could also tell during the time the rape was taking place that the someone was wearing a flannel shirt.

I can vividly remember squeezing my eyes shut as tightly as I could underneath the pillowcase, even though I was unable to see through it. I felt certain by that someone's threatening and hostile demeanor that, if he thought for a moment that I could see his face, he would make sure I didn't live to describe it to anyone. I had difficulty breathing underneath the pillowcase, yet I considered it a blessing that it covered my eyes so that I would not have to visualize what was about to take place.

Even though I had been ordered to get on my knees, I was paralyzed, unable to move. While referring to me as "bitch," the someone then grabbed me by my shoulders and shoved me down to the floor. He lifted the pillowcase up from my chin just far enough to expose the area of my mouth and ordered me to open. As the night progressed, with every command, that certain someone's mannerisms escalated, becoming more and more violent. He became angrier and cruel, leaving me with the feeling I was going to be killed after he finished what he came there to do.

Prior to that horrendous night, I had never been exposed to oral sex.

Throughout the time the oral sex was taking place, the someone continued to verbally insult and humiliate me with language such as, "Suck it," and, "Don't bite it," while at the same time constantly referring to me as "bitch." It was clear that the use of such language was a personal signature of that certain someone as a means to further demean and degrade his victims. To this day, I feel certain that the anger and hostility displayed by that certain someone did not just vanish after that night and that, more likely than not, there have been other victims of his abuse. That thought alone makes the treatment I received from local law enforcement following the rape all the more despicable.

Any physical movement forward on my part was forced and robotic, void of any humanistic feeling. I could feel the person I once was slowly disintegrating, seeping into nothingness. The events that occurred on that night are permanently inked in my mind and will remain forever, tormenting and haunting me whether I am awake or asleep.

When that someone had finished with his oral degradation, with tremendous brute force, he jerked me up from my knees by my shoulders and ordered me to take off my clothes. After my clothes were removed, the someone shoved me backward onto the bed, ordering me to turn over onto my stomach. He then took the other pillowcase from my bed and tied my hands behind my back. I don't know why, but it was at this particular moment I was convinced that he was going to kill me by shooting me in the back of my head. It is almost impossible to describe the emotions and the vulnerability one feels when lying naked, face down, with your hands tied behind your back.

So strong was my feeling that he was about to kill me that I began to beg him not to. He angrily responded, *"I ain't gonna kill you!"* He then flung me back over onto my back, attempting to get on top of me. I couldn't lie down flat because my hands were tied behind me, so he struggled to get on top of me. He kept pushing me backward while at the same time continuing his attempts to get on top of me. I told the someone I couldn't lie backward with my hands tied behind me. Clearly disgusted and annoyed, the someone then mumbled inaudible words under his breath while flinging me back over onto my stomach a second time. He untied my hands, then flipped me back on my back again.

After that certain someone had finished raping me, it seemed as if he was drifting in and out of this bizarre metamorphosis. He appeared to become this cynical, overgrown child, acting giddy and jovial. Then came yet another change, seemingly by habit, back into his prior morbid, devious, and deranged personality. It was as if he was now gloating in his conquering abilities and the complete control he had over his prey, so much so that he actually began laughing out loud! I have often wondered how many times that certain someone had performed this abominable routine on others.

The someone then jokingly said, "You fool; it was so easy to get in." He had breached my home easily undetected. The statement was a means not only to further humiliate me but to also make me feel ignorant that I hadn't foreseen this happening. When he finished his juvenile, ridiculing, and belittling production, he got up from the bed and flung me over onto my stomach again. He tied my hands behind my back again then asked if I had only the one telephone. Although I answered yes, he left the bedroom, and I could hear him walking through the house, checking just to be sure.

Chapter Eight:
Warnings and Threats

After walking through the house, the someone returned to the bedroom, blurting out the words, "I'll be outside watching for five minutes, and you better not do anything," which was followed by, "If I see a light come on in here before five minutes are up, I'll come back and cut your guts out!" I was 100 percent certain that, if I did not do exactly as he said, he would come back and do just that.

As I continued lying naked on the bed with the pillowcase covering my head and my hands tied behind me, there came a point when I heard the back door open and close. I lay there for what felt like five minutes while at the same time trying to wrestle my hands free. When a feeling of adrenaline raged through my body, I was able to free my hands, and in a panic-stricken fog, I threw on clothes, grabbed my keys and pocketbook, and flew out the front door, all the time not knowing whether that certain someone was waiting for me outside as he had threatened.

When I was able to make it to my car and lock myself in, then and only then did the hysterical screaming and sobbing emitting from a soul scarcely remaining begin to bellow all throughout the car. This was followed by uncontrollable physical shaking and all-over chills.

Chapter Nine:
Finding Shelter

I do not recall how long I remained in that state, sitting in my car, nor do I recall the point when I turned on the ignition. Thoughts and emotions were everywhere, yet nowhere; the only thing I could rationalize was that I had to get to my parents' house. Thinking back, it seemed ironic that I couldn't wait to leave my parents' home when I grew up, and now at this moment in time, I was frantically striving to find my way back.

For reasons unknown, I set out in the wrong direction while fleeing the neighborhood. At a certain point, I saw an individual standing outside the front door of a house. Shockingly, I stopped my car and jumped out into the middle of the street, screaming, "I've been raped!" I realized much later how insane that maneuver was, since for all I knew, he could have been the rapist! I don't know how long I stood there in the road screaming and sobbing, but when I started to get back into my car, I couldn't open the door. In my outlandish state of uncontrolled frenzy, I had locked my keys inside the car! The individual previously standing outside the home retrieved a clothes hanger from inside and used it to open my car door. I jumped in as soon as he opened it and sped away. The next thing I recalled was being on the front porch of my parents' home, screaming and banging on their front door—I've never actually known how I got there.

While I was banging on the door at my parents' home, I could see through the glass panes that my daddy was bolting toward the door, gun in hand, Mama following closely behind. When Daddy saw who was banging on the door, he slung it open, and I stumbled in, practically falling into his arms screaming, "I've been raped!"

My mama let out a bone-chilling scream while Daddy continued to stand in the door to keep me from falling. After a few seconds had passed, I felt my daddy's arms fall to his sides as he handed me over to my mama. Then Mama and I watched my daddy slowly walk, as if he were in a hazy fog, toward that same landline telephone located in the main room of their house to call the police. While Daddy was on the telephone, Mama took me and sat me down on the bed in the front bedroom, the same bedroom that my sister and I shared all the years we were growing up. Mama slowly sat down right next to me, both of us crying and sobbing, awaiting the arrival of the police.

Mama and I rode in the police car to Gaston Memorial Hospital, as it was known at that time, with Daddy following behind in his car. During the ride in the police car, the officer immediately began asking me questions about the rape. As I began providing some of the details, Mama started screaming again; she just couldn't take it. I told the officer the questions would have to wait until later when Mama wasn't present. A physical examination and rape-kit collection at the hospital followed—which, by the way, was a type of humiliation all its own, as in, my opinion was met with cold, heartless, and dismissive stares on the part of the medical staff.

While at the hospital, I asked my Mama to call my husband and let him know what had happened, even though we were separated at the time. My mama did so reluctantly, as both she and my Daddy were of the opinion that he could have orchestrated the break-in and assault. He didn't come up to the hospital to check on me that night, nor did he ever ask me any questions whatsoever about the incident afterward. My Daddy specifically asked the police to question him about the incident at the time; however (according to him), they never did. Shortly thereafter, he left the area and moved to Canada.

After being discharged from the hospital, I was released into the care of my parents and thereafter moved back into their home.

PART III: PROCESSING, COPING, AND ADVOCATING FOR MYSELF

Chapter Ten:
The Aftermath and the Rapist's Return

After the rape, I obviously could not return to my home, so I moved back in with my parents. It felt as if I had shell shock, having to survive one day at a time with a radically altered personality that floundered between fear, sorrow, guilt, bitterness, and hate, along with the "Why me?" question always looming silently in my head. There was also a mountain of never-before-experienced characteristics being exerted at that time. I no longer knew who, or even what, I was with this now total stranger living in the body I previously occupied.

I was forced to undergo extensive psychological counseling and prescribed antidepressant medications then and all throughout the years following for acute depression, anxiety, and post-traumatic stress disorder. In addition, the family dynamics I previously shared with my parents and siblings were never the same, even though I was back at home. For a time, I felt that my family members struggled with what to say or how to act while in my presence. I didn't feel like I belonged to them anymore. There were numerous times I would break down sobbing at a moment's notice and have to flee to the safety of my childhood bedroom. I cried throughout the days and nights, and there was also an episode of sleepwalking. My mama told me that I walked into her and Daddy's bedroom and kept repeating, "Are you through?" She said she could tell I was asleep, so she gently put me back to bed.

I felt as if everything I had experienced in my life from birth up until that point was counterfeit. I also suffered from extreme guilt that I had brought all this pain and suffering into my parents' lives, something they never dreamed could happen. I felt petty, distant, and ashamed that my family suffered throughout their entire lives because of what that someone had done not only to me but, in a sense, to them as well.

I know my daddy especially was greatly impacted by the event and also the fact that the local law enforcement office was doing absolutely nothing to try to identify and arrest that certain someone who was responsible for it all. I knew the kind of man my daddy was and knew he was living in misery because he couldn't do anything to help me. I had begun to feel like a child meeting their new adoptive parents for the first time, each of us beginning the steps necessary to start our lives anew with each other.

As a constant reminder throughout this time as well as the following years, always in the background of everyone's mind in my family was the fact that the rapist had never been arrested and was still out there somewhere. It is commonly known that a rapist doesn't just stop what he's doing overnight, and again, I feel certain that there had been previous rapes committed by that same certain someone as well as afterward.

One would assume that if that certain someone was fortunate enough to avoid being arrested for such a crime, the first item on the agenda would be to flee from the area and disappear. The rapist in my case would boldly dispel that assumption by repeatedly returning to the scene of the crime! After all, my home stood vacant immediately following the rape until it could be sold.

It was glaringly evident that this someone had no fear of being arrested and just decided to make himself right at home in my house! He continued to torment me by subsequently breaking and entering and, now, helping himself to the personal property that remained inside my home, property that I was never able to recover. My family and I would discover his additional break-ins at various times when we went to collect items of my personal property. He flaunted his occasional presence by leaving his signature odor of cigarettes, which stagnantly lingered all through the house. He also used the bathroom while he was there, urinating in the toilet and tossing his cigarette butts in!

It seemed as though that certain someone was still laughing about how easy it was to break into my home, and worse was the fact that the local law enforcement office didn't seem to care.

Chapter Eleven:
The Investigation That Wasn't

I never understood how or why rape at gunpoint, along with additional crimes of break-ins and larceny, would not warrant a criminal investigation. If an arrest could not be made for the rape at that point in time, then surely an arrest for the subsequent break-ins and larcenies could be pursued. In my case, there were no arrests for any of the crimes committed against me by that certain someone.

I recall numerous occasions immediately after the rape and the years that followed that I and/or Daddy would contact the police department inquiring as to their investigation. We received only various excuses, such as someone would get back with us or the case was still pending, and later on, we were advised that the file could not be located. I recall one occasion in particular when I called, and an officer advised me that since the rape didn't result in a murder, they were not required to keep the file or that the file had been destroyed. The officer further stated that I "just needed to forget about it all, move on, and get closure." Another time, I contacted the Gaston County DA's office requesting that they check into my case. I was advised by their office that if I would have the police department send my file over to them, they would reopen the case. Needless to say, even though I relayed this information to the police department, they never forwarded the case file over to the DA's office.

Later, when DNA was being used to solve old cold cases, I contacted the police department and requested that the rape-kit evidence their office received from the hospital on the night I was attacked be submitted for DNA testing. I just assumed that evidence collected in a criminal case entrusted to the care of the police department would be preserved in the event additional information and/or evidence was obtained in the future. During this time, I was advised by the police department that my file could not be located but that they would continue to look for it and get back with me. As was the case numerous times in the past, that never happened.

It was not until 2017, after yet another call attempting to have my case reopened, that an officer who actually took the time to try to locate my file succeeded. What was located was only a thin shell of a file, containing very limited information taken immediately following the rape, and it contained scarcely any additional information added thereafter. The officer advised that, after a thorough search, no additional information could be located. I began to feel as though I had been raped all over again, this time by law enforcement.

This meant that all of the evidence, which was substantial, that had been collected on the night of the rape, including the rape-kit evidence, had either been lost, thrown away, or destroyed!

All of this seemed incredible to me, since I was advised that in North Carolina, there was no statute of limitations on my case. I remember thinking that had the case file never been located and, further, had I not on my own obtained a copy of my hospital records from the night of the rape, there would never have been any record that the rape even occurred!

I recall one officer making the cold statement to me that "I should be glad the rapist didn't kill me." I guess that if I had, in fact, been killed by that certain someone, then maybe the police would have at least investigated the case on behalf of my parents.

In 2017, for the first time, I was able to view what was left of the contents of my case file; it contained a basic typed report of the rape along with an inaccurate handwritten statement prepared by a police officer. Also, and more importantly, contained in the case file was the SBI lab's *typed* report reflecting their findings from my rape-kit evidence, initially submitted to their office by the police department following the attack. There were no entries in the case file relating to the subsequent break-ins and larceny nor any indication that my neighbors had been questioned by the police the night of the rape as my daddy had requested. I remember Daddy calling the police department, advising them that the rapist was returning to the scene of the crime, breaking in again and again and stealing my personal property. Daddy requested that a police officer stake out the home a couple of nights, and they would be able to make an arrest. Of course, that request fell on deaf ears.

My family and I never received any information from the police department concerning my case. Painfully frustrated with the attitude put forth by the local police department, my daddy finally advised me that "we might as well forget about them helping us, because they're not." Daddy was angry and at the same time heartbroken at the total lack of concern by the police department, especially since there was an armed rapist still out there on the streets of the city. We were made to feel as though my case was of no consequence, even though it involved a vicious crime involving the use of a deadly weapon, and there was also the public's safety at issue with regard to this criminal. It was always Daddy or me who called for information and/or left numerous messages with the police in an attempt to find out the status of their investigation, all to no avail.

Even the actions of the various police officers on the night of the rape were telling in that certain questions asked by the officers made me feel as though I had done something to cause the rape. Their attitudes were cold, almost to the point of being callous, the entire time. I began to experience that animosity-toward-women-in-general attitude all over again. I was also provided with the name of a female police officer on the force who would be contacting me about my case. I never heard from her. It was as if the police didn't consider what happened to me to even be a crime!

In the years that followed, I contacted an individual who lived in the neighborhood where the rape occurred, and almost immediately, I detected a certain amount of resistance from that individual to discuss the event with me. (I think I know the reason why.) It was not until I told her I just wanted to thank the individual who helped me unlock my car that night that she finally agreed to provide me with his name. His name was Allen, but she said she didn't know his last name. (I knew this was not the case.) In any event, she went on to state that Allen had since died but that he had previously told her about it and told her that I ran out into the street that night. She went on to add that no one else had ever mentioned a word about it to her. If she was being truthful, this confirmed that the police had not questioned the neighbors who lived close by, as my daddy and I had previously requested.

Chapter Twelve:
Family Intervention

When my family and I finally accepted the fact that the police were not going to investigate my rape case nor the continued break-ins and thefts, my daddy felt he could not just sit back, accept what had happened, and do nothing. He made the decision to perform his own stakeouts in an attempt to catch the rapist on his own. On these family stakeouts, Mama would prepare large thermoses of black coffee to accompany Daddy and other family members to help them stay awake during the long nights waiting for the rapist to return.

On the nights of my family's stakeouts, oddly enough, that certain someone didn't return, but he would show up on the occasions when they weren't there. This confirmed to us that the certain someone lived close enough to be able to see when family members were being dropped off and picked up at the residence. This would tend to make sense also due to the fact that the someone made use of nearby items (cement blocks, trash can, etc.) while breaking in.

My parents have long since passed away at the time of the writing of this memoir. How sad it was that they were the only ones, other than me and other family members, interested in bringing a rapist to justice—not only for me but for others who more than likely have been victims of that same certain someone as well. This type of crime is extremely difficult for the parents, as they want to be able to help their loved one, but the truth is, there's nothing they can do. I will never forget the look on my parents' faces the night they initially learned what had happened to their daughter.

Chapter Thirteen:
My Research

There were various times through the years that I went to the local library to view old Gaston County newspaper articles to see if there had been other sexual assaults in Gaston County that may have been reported to the local police around that time.

I located an article dated approximately two years after my rape reflecting two additional rapes that had been reported. The father of one of the rape victims contacted the newspaper expressing his anger concerning the way his daughter's case was handled by the same police department. The victim's father indicated that his daughter's case was being treated as a joke, as if her rape had not actually happened. (I could certainly relate.) He further indicated that he felt they were trying to make his daughter look like the culprit. I wish I could have located those victims to see if there were any similarities between their cases and mine; unfortunately, I was never able to obtain any contact information for those individuals.

I have expended numerous hours over the years attempting to investigate my own case, but as a layperson having minimal resources to work with, not to mention the fact that my case file could not be located for so many years, I had little to no chance of obtaining information that may have been helpful in solving my case.

Chapter Fourteen:
Evidence

According to the records from the hospital, the rape-kit evidence given to the police department on the night of my attack consisted of the collection of seminal fluid, pubic hair–collection lifter, pubic hair collection, and two slides of vaginal secretions. Also collected on the night of the rape by the police department were various items of bedding, including my pillowcases, one of which was still tied at both ends forming a loop, my underwear, and my bedroom slippers. The police also dusted for and lifted fingerprints from the residence and took photographs of the interior and exterior of the house that night.

In accordance with the SBI lab's typed report that was still in my case file as of 2017, the subject report reflected that DNA evidence from that certain someone was indeed obtained and confirmed by the SBI lab's report. The police department never notified me, nor my family, of those results, nor were we ever advised of the results of any of the other evidence collected that night. There was no indication in the case file that any follow-ups or investigations had been performed by the police department as a result of the rape, nor any follow-ups with the SBI lab regarding their findings.

Chapter Fifteen: Perseverance

According to various articles in the local newspaper around the time I was raped, there appeared to be substantial municipal issues going on between the city and county. As reflected in those articles, there were, specifically, conflicts and turmoil going on between the police department and the sheriff's office with threats of walkouts. This could possibly explain the reason why my rape case was handled in the manner it was. The articles also reflected there were murders, drug wars, motorcycle-group conflicts, club wars, thefts, music-video piracy, robberies, and B and Es going on during that time. The articles further reflected that five of the six detectives were investigating a murder case at the time.

As a result of the crimes, chaos, and discord going on in the area, I guess the police were of the opinion that even though I was raped at gunpoint, my case did not rise to the level deemed necessary to warrant investigation, protection, or justice in general for me and other potential victims of that certain someone. I couldn't help but think that had

I not been fortunate enough to have family members living nearby with whom I could stay following the rape, I would have been forced to return to my home, allowing that certain someone the opportunity to rape again, since he kept returning to my home.

Other newspaper articles I researched during that time reflected break-ins and sexual assaults: eight break-ins that year between Monday on New Year's Eve to the following Wednesday, with my case bringing that total to nine. I would comb through city directories and old telephone books at the library, again trying to investigate my own case, in an attempt to obtain contact information for individuals that lived in the neighborhood at that time who may have some information, all to no avail. I also placed various ads on Craigslist trying to locate individuals and/or information, again without any success. I did however receive some strange responses to those ads at times.

As the years passed on, I would not give up and continuously pursued the reopening of my case with the police department. Eventually, with the location of my case file, I finally began to have hope that with all the evidence that had been collected, specifically the rape-kit evidence, DNA testing could now be performed and hopefully bring that certain someone to justice, or at least reveal his identity. As I have discussed, I naively just assumed that evidence collected in a criminal case entrusted to the care of the police department would be preserved in the event additional information were to be obtained in the future. It was not until 2017 when my case file was finally located that I learned that *none* of the evidence collected by the police department in my case could be located, and more than likely, it had been lost, discarded, or destroyed. All hopes of ever bringing that certain someone to justice—and perhaps protecting other potential victims as well— gone. As of the writing of this memoir, there is no pending investigation in my case since no evidence now exists to move forward.

Chapter Sixteen: After the Aftermath

The events surrounding my rape had never been printed in the newspaper, as at the time of the rape, my Daddy had specifically requested of the police that the assault not be reported, so at one point some years later, I contacted our local newspaper requesting that my story be printed in the hope that there might be someone who had information that might be helpful in my case. The reporter that I spoke with agreed, and we discussed that the story would be aired in the news via videotape and that my face would be shaded for safety reasons. In advance of the making of the video, I spent a considerable amount of time preparing the statement I was going to read, outlining the facts and circumstances of the case, and later, I made an appointment to meet with the reporter for the recording. We subsequently made the video recording, and the reporter provided me with the date my story would air. I contacted my family members and provided them with the date as well.

To my surprise, the date my video recording was to air came and went, minus my story!

I telephoned the reporter the next day to inquire what happened, to which he responded, "It got bumped." I asked him what he meant, and his explanation was that another story aired in its place. I waited for him to provide me with an alternate date for the story to air, but I was met with silence on the other end of the telephone. That was the last conversation I had with the reporter, and my story never aired. The reporter never gave me a copy of the video, even though it contained all of my personal information.

Chapter Seventeen:
Law Enforcement's Role

It was clear early on that law enforcement was not interested in taking my case seriously and made it appear as though I had done something wrong or had done something to provoke the attack. On the night I was raped, I was subjected to accusatory remarks from some of the police officers, such as, "You don't walk around with your curtains open and no clothes on, do you?" and, "Do you always leave your underwear lying out all over the place like this?"—a reference to the damp laundry I had placed on my ironing board to finish drying during the night.

I came across a news article from 2013 wherein an individual known as the ski mask rapist was arrested for the rape of several women in the Mecklenburg County area, which is very close to Gaston County, in the late 1970s. I reached out to the news station who reported on the article to inquire about that individual and explained the circumstances of my case since my rapist wore a ski mask as well. The reporter from Mecklenburg County requested that she be allowed to report on my case. I agreed, and the article concerning my story ran in January of 2017. The reporter also contacted the police department to make an inquiry on my case and actually spoke with an investigator who advised her that they "will take another look at the case"—which, again, never happened. (The information containing my story is in the reporter's news article, reflected as updated, dated January 4, 2017.)

The article further reflected that said investigator advised her that there was no statute of limitations in my case, and upon the reporter's inquiry concerning DNA evidence, the investigator advised her there wasn't any with the case file. To elaborate on the investigator's statement, his response was accurate as to actual physical evidence. However, there does exist a typed report in my case file from the SBI lab in Raleigh, North Carolina, confirming the existence of that someone's DNA, as I have mentioned. The sad part is that since the police department lost or destroyed the original rape-kit slides that contained the actual physical evidence, additional recent and further DNA testing can not be performed.

I was later advised by the local police department that their comparison between the ski mask rapist's case and mine were not related.

After the Mecklenburg County news article was printed, I received a call from a reporter in my county, who, after reading the Mecklenburg County article, requested that she also be allowed to run a news article concerning my case. I assumed this interest was due to the fact that my case dealt with an incident that occurred in Gaston County. Ironically, this was the same newspaper that never aired the videotaped version of my story previously—the one that "got bumped."

After reading the second news article prepared by the reporter in my county dated January 9, 2017, I was quite taken aback. In my opinion, it was poorly worded, with some of the contents comprised from the prior news article from Mecklenburg County. It also contained errors and information that did not originate with me. In my opinion, the article came across as a random story written in the form of a novel and seemed as though the second reporter inserted her own wording and circumstances to embellish her version of my story.

Chapter Eighteen: Security Advice

As a result of my prior naivete, I was completely unaware of the risks women take when living alone. I found out that these types of someones are always out there stalking their victims for some time in order to determine their daily routine and habits, just watching and waiting for the perfect opportunity to make their move.

I once had a conversation with a detective who made the statement to me that he felt that "ninety percent of the world we live in are animals," and at that time, I can truly say I believed it. The detective also stated that, if women were going to be living alone, they needed to be able to protect themselves. In his candidness, which I welcomed, he advised that if they were contemplating the use of a weapon, he would not recommend a handgun for home protection but rather a loaded shotgun kept in the corner beside your bed if possible. (Of course, this was if living alone and there were no children in the home.) The reasoning was that in the event a rape situation arises, fear and emotions are running high, and if you have a handgun, you're going to be scared and nervous and your hands will be shaking; if you missed, the criminal would be angry and become more violent. If, on the other hand, you have a shotgun, he said, you just reach out, grab it, swing it around, and "he's all over the wall!"

That certain someone in my case will never know how close he came to being all over the wall, so to speak, during the times he kept returning to the scene of the crime when my daddy was doing his stakeouts.

That same detective was of the opinion that the certain someone in my case had been watching me for a while prior to breaking in, that he had my daily routine down and knew I lived alone. He also indicated that the guy had probably raped before since everything he did seemed so organized and planned out. He went on to say that it was highly possible that the someone had gotten into my home previously to get the layout of the inside then came back on the night he decided to commit the rape, thus keeping him from bumping into furniture.

PART IV: A NEW SELF

Chapter Nineteen: A Different Life

That certain someone did not take my life that night, for which I am very thankful; however, my life was drastically changed and replaced with a *different* life that began immediately following that New Year's Eve in 1978. I wholeheartedly became a different individual, with whom I had to learn to live with, whether I liked that individual or not. There were numerous times throughout the years that I can honestly say I did not like this new individual, and I doubt anyone else around me at the time did either.

Chapter Twenty: A Day in the Life of a Rape Victim

The physical and psychological trauma forced upon a rape victim always remains and becomes a part of the individual. As she attempts to carry on with life and daily routines, there will always be that trigger potential that will painfully set into motion the event as if it is occurring all over again.

A victim of rape suffers from fear that the rapist will someday return and is constantly looking out windows, repeatedly checking to make sure that the doors she just locked the previous three times are still locked. There is the fear of no longer being able to live a normal life or have a normal relationship with someone, and at times, she just wants to disappear completely. The worries of never being able to sleep soundly again and no longer feeling safe are constant. When out in public, she's constantly looking around, feeling panicky if someone veers too close in her vicinity. She always thinks if a stranger approaches and speaks to her, "Could this be him?" She also worries about whether she can ever be brave enough to live on her own again and always agonizes over "Why me?"

The thoughts and emotions expressed in this memoir represent a menial attempt by me personally to somewhat articulate the mental and physical trauma I endured as a rape victim. It remains a permanent, debilitating trauma that never goes away, making closure impossible. A rapist will go on with his life as if he has done nothing wrong, while his victim will be reminded of the horror of his actions for the rest of hers.

Chapter Twenty-One:
Reporting Crimes of Rape

With the rapid and ongoing advances in DNA evidence, which includes family genealogy now, the identity of criminals can be obtained, even if the crimes occurred decades ago, so there is no need to ever give up thinking that a case can't be solved. There may be women who have been raped and for various reasons never reported those rapes to law enforcement. I am encouraging everyone to come forward and report those cases to law enforcement. In doing so, you just may be preventing certain someones from moving on to their next victim.

I also want to encourage everyone to be proactive in their cases of rape, in seeing that the cases are actually being investigated and followed up on by law enforcement. These types of crimes usually involve additional crimes, such as breaking and entering and theft, that can also be prosecuted. By being proactive in these types of criminal cases, you will be sending a strong message to law enforcement and, more importantly, to the criminals themselves that all legal remedies will be utilized in order to obtain the justice that the victims are entitled to and greatly deserve.

This will also continue keeping these types of cases before the public to shed light on just how frequently these crimes occur. I would like to add also that the victims should never be afraid to call and check on the status of their cases often, and if necessary, make an appointment to meet with the officer in charge of investigating the case to discuss its progress.

I also hope that by sharing my story, it will serve as a reminder to others that they should utilize whatever security measures are available to them if they plan to live alone. A simple plan such as just having a dog can be an advantage, who just by barking may serve as a deterrent to that certain someone who may be contemplating a break-in.

I hope that my story may also serve as a reminder to others that the light at the end of *their* journey's tunnel is there, and that *their* story, should they desire to share it, may help others that have gone through or are going through similar circumstances.

Chapter Twenty-Two:
Journey to Recovery

My personal journey toward recovery was met with ongoing nightmares, sleepless nights, tears, depression, anxiety, PTSD, counseling, medications, failed relationships and marriages, continuous questioning of "Why me?", bitterness, and self-pity. I was fortunate enough, however, to have been involved in church while growing up, and although I didn't know a lot about God at the time, I knew that since I was allowed to live through that night, I would be given the means to overcome the events that occurred.

I was finally able to come to terms with and accept the person that I ultimately became and actually became a much stronger individual than before. I also received the strength necessary to break free from the control I was at one time allowing that certain someone to have over me. I have long since forgiven that someone for his actions, knowing that he will have to give an account for them to our Heavenly Father.

My life's journey would subsequently result in a rewarding career as a certified paralegal and notary public for North Carolina, a real estate signing agent, and a board director for a homeowner's association. My journey would also result in the births of three beautiful children, along with the births of four precious grandchildren. I was able to regain the independence and security that was so willfully taken from me that night, and I no longer live in fear.

Chapter Twenty-Three:
Sharing My Story

I wanted to share my story in order to bring to light the various issues with law enforcement that I and my family had to endure in the hopes that it will never happen to anyone else and, specifically, to bring to light the duty of law enforcement to protect and to preserve evidence entrusted to their care in a criminal case.

As long as I remain living, I feel I owe it to my family and other potential rape victims to never give up trying to obtain the identity of that certain someone. Perhaps someday an acquaintance or friend of his may be willing to share information now that so many years have passed.

I hope that the sharing of my story may serve as a means of encouragement to other victims who have suffered similar crimes or that may, heaven forbid, endure similar circumstances in the future. Again, I can't stress enough the need to report crimes of rape. In doing so, it may prevent the same thing from happening to a friend or loved one. If sexual assaults are not reported, it leaves the door open for all the other evil someones running around out there to continue on to their next victim. The public needs to be kept advised on just how frequently these crimes occur, which in turn will pressure law enforcement agencies and other state offices and officials to see to it that these cases are swiftly and thoroughly investigated and evidence preserved. At times there may be cases and circumstances wherein a rapist gets away with his crime; however, they may not be so lucky a second time.

I also hope that the facts and circumstances of my case may someday be compared and evaluated with other law enforcement agencies for similarities in other cases of rape. Additionally, if through my continued efforts and pursuits I can be of assistance in seeing that the certain someone never has an opportunity to do to another individual what he did to me, then the lack of action in the handling of my case by law enforcement will not have been in vain.

I'm hoping also that in sharing my experience, it may help to remind others that rape victims are made to suffer permanent, debilitating mental and emotional trauma that will affect them for the rest of their lives, whether the rapist is prosecuted or not. Even in cases where the rapist has been identified, arrested, and punished for their crimes, in the mind of the victim, her case will never be closed.

It is also my sincere hope that in the future, law enforcement in the various cities and states will become more proactive in their investigation of these types of cases and investigate them on a case-by-case basis, swiftly and competently. The officers should be properly trained in the investigation process of dealing with these specific types of crimes against women and the ongoing horror and impact it has on family members as well. Please keep in mind also that some states have statutes of limitation, which limit the time in which these cases can be prosecuted, so again, victims need to stay on top of their respective cases to make sure they do not slip through the cracks, resulting in evidence lost or destroyed, as was the case in my circumstance.

Finally, a very important factor to remember is that if an individual elects to obtain a weapon of any kind for home-security reasons, they should always go through the necessary training as to its use and more importantly making sure the weapon is properly stored and out of the reach of children.

Dedication

This memoir is dedicated to my parents, Lamar and Julia Russell, for loving and supporting me always, along with my sister Lawana, my brothers Kevin and Joel, and numerous other family members and friends. This memoir is also dedicated with much love to my children, Tara Hovis, Cole, and Taylor Patton, and my precious grandchildren, Cameron, Brandon, Bella, and Chelsea Patton.

I would also like to thank the sergeant with the Gaston County Police Department who in the latter years cared enough to actually search for and locate my case file, thereby confirming its existence.

Most importantly, this memoir is dedicated to the One who gave me the faith and strength I would need to overcome the obstacles faced along the pathway of my life, not only for the events of that horrific night but also through my diagnosis of breast cancer in April 2019. God is the reason I am still here to be able to share my story with others, a living testimony of God's grace and undying love for one of His children.

Romans 8:38–39 of the KJV Bible reads as follows: "For I am persuaded that neither death nor life, nor angels nor principalities, nor powers, nor things present, nor things to come, nor height, nor depth, nor any other creature, shall be able to separate us from the love of God which is in Christ Jesus our Lord." With this knowledge, I will not fear what man (*or any certain someone*) shall do to me. Jesus said, "I am the Root and the Offspring of David and the Bright and Morning Star." He always was and still is the light that has shone and still shines in what I deem as my life's journey.